THE GRACE OF GIVING

MONEY AND THE GOSPEL

INCLUDES

THE GIFT OF ACCOUNTABILITY

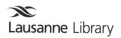
Lausanne Library

THE GRACE OF GIVING

MONEY AND THE GOSPEL

—————— INCLUDES ——————

THE GIFT OF ACCOUNTABILITY

JOHN STOTT & CHRIS WRIGHT
FOREWORD BY FEMI B ADELEYE

The Grace of Giving: Money and the Gospel

Hendrickson Publishers Marketing, LLC
P. O. Box 3473
Peabody, Massachusetts 01961-3473

This booklet arose from an exposition by John Stott of 2 Corinthians 8 & 9 entitled Ten Principles of Christian Giving. It was delivered first at The Gathering in San Diego in 1998, and later repeated at All Souls Church, Langham Place, London. It was first published in the USA in 2003 by Generous Giving and is reproduced here, slightly expanded, by kind permission of the author.

ISBN 978-1-61970-764-1

Printed in the United States of America

Second Printing—April 2019

Royalties have kindly been donated to support the publishing ministry of the Lausanne Movement.

Cover design by John Ruffin

Contents

The Gift of Accountability
Chris Wright

Foreword

This is an unusual little volume. Two writers look at the same passages from the Apostle Paul, and draw out complementary principles on handling money. John Stott focuses on Paul's teaching on giving, Chris Wright on accountability. I can testify to the personal integrity of both authors; and to their deep desire not only to live by these principles, but to share them in a relevant way with God's people around the world.

We need to see our giving as a response to God's own generosity. There is a pastoral feel to John Stott's writing—sometimes, as he says, it may be right to reduce our giving. We should always give thoughtfully, and keep our giving under review.

Churches tend to associate Paul's teaching here only with a call to give. I hope this short book will help to change that, for these scriptures teach much more. The six principles of accountability that Chris Wright highlights are non-negotiable. A safety-net of accountability is critical for those in positions of responsibility, to whom money has been entrusted.

Many will be surprised by Chris's assertion that, on the plain level of number of verses, the Apostle Paul 'gives more text space to writing about issues relating to financial affairs of churches than he does to writing about justification by faith.' The spiritual nature of this subject is clear, and the Apostle's theology of money, as God-centred and mission-centred, deserves keen attention.

We shall all be shaped by either the values society imposes on us, or by the biblical principles clearly articulated here. So we need to consider Paul's teaching closely. I commend the words of John Stott and Chris Wright as they challenge us to be more deliberate in engaging with this subject, as part of a God-focused, Christ-centred and spirit-led life.

Femi B. Adeleye
Associate Director (Africa), Langham Preaching,
Langham Partnership
Member: Lausanne Movement Board

THE GRACE
OF GIVING

John Stott

Introduction

When we become Christians, our giving has a new impetus. We are called to give generously, and with joy, as a fruit of the Spirit's life within us. The following pages take us through the Apostle Paul's teaching on Christian giving, and draw out principles which we can apply to our own situation. I trust you will find it a helpful and provocative study, as I have found it to be myself.

In 2 Corinthians 8 & 9, Paul is explaining arrangements for an offering from the Greek churches of Achaia and Macedonia for the impoverished churches of Judea. We also read about it in Romans 15 and 1 Corinthians 16. Paul did not see giving as a mundane matter, nor as something on the periphery of church life. On the contrary, he saw the grace of giving as a core part of what it means for us to be members of Christ's Church.

He shows how our regular giving is rooted in three central themes in the gospel: the grace of God, the cross of Christ, and the unity of the Spirit. It is very moving to grasp this combination of profound Trinitarian theology and practical common sense, as we shall see.

Here are Paul's ten principles. We start at the beginning of 2 Corinthians 8.

1

Christian giving is an expression of the grace of God (2 Corinthians 8:1–6)

And now, brothers, we want you to know about the grace that God has given the Macedonian churches. ²Out of the most severe trial, their overflowing joy and their extreme poverty welled up in rich generosity. ³For I testify that they gave as much as they were able, and even beyond their ability. Entirely on their own, ⁴they urgently pleaded with us for the privilege of sharing in this service to the saints. ⁵And they did not do as we expected, but they gave themselves first to the Lord and then to us in keeping with God's will. ⁶So we urged Titus, since he had earlier made a beginning, to bring also to completion this act of grace on your part.

Paul does not begin by referring to the generosity of the churches of Macedonia in northern Greece. He starts instead with 'the grace which God has given to the Macedonian churches' (v1). Grace is another word for generosity. In other words, behind the generosity of Macedonia, Paul saw the generosity of God. Our gracious God is a generous God, and he is at work in his people to make them generous too.

Three tributaries come together in the river of Macedonian generosity, namely their severe trial, their overflowing joy and their extreme poverty (v2). In consequence, the Macedonians gave even beyond their ability (v3), and they pleaded for the privilege of doing so (v4). How easily our comfortable western culture can deaden our sensitivity to others' needs. The Macedonians had no such comfort, and no such lure of personal satisfaction. Their values were entirely different. They gave themselves first to the Lord, and then to Paul and his fellow workers (v5). What a model for the Corinthians, and for us.

We read next how Paul had urged Titus to complete what he had begun in Corinth, the capital of Achaia, some time before (v6). What had Titus begun? He had been exhorting the Corinthians to give in the same way as the Macedonians.

This then is where Paul begins—with the grace of God in the Macedonian churches of northern Greece and with the same grace of God in the Achaian churches of southern Greece. Their Christian generosity is an outflow of the generosity of God.

2

Christian giving can be a *charisma*, that is a gift of the Spirit (8:7)

[7]But just as you excel in everything—in faith, in speech, in knowledge, in complete earnestness and in your love for us—see that you also excel in this grace of giving.

The Corinthians already excel in the spiritual gifts of faith, speech, knowledge, earnestness and love, and the apostle urges them to excel also 'in this grace of giving'. Similarly in Romans 12:8 Paul includes among another list of *charismata* 'contributing to the needs of others'. The grace of giving is a spiritual gift.

Many of God's gifts are generously bestowed in some measure on all believers and given in special measure to some. For example, all Christians are called to share the gospel with others, but some have the gift of an evangelist. All Christians are called to exercise pastoral care for others, but some are called to be pastors. Just so, all

Christians are called to be generous, but some are given the particular 'gift of giving'. Those entrusted with significant financial resources have a special responsibility to be good stewards of those resources.

3

Christian giving is inspired by the cross of Christ (8:8,9)

> *⁸I am not commanding you, but I want to test the sincerity of your love by comparing it with the earnestness of others. ⁹For you know the grace of our Lord Jesus Christ, that though he was rich, yet for your sakes he became poor, so that you through his poverty might become rich.*

Paul was not commanding the Corinthians to give generously. This is not how he deals with them. Rather he puts the sincerity of their love to the test by comparing them with others and especially (it is implied) with Christ. For they knew 'the grace of our Lord Jesus Christ'.

Let us note this further reference to divine grace. The grace of God is at work in us (v1), and the grace of Christ challenges us to respond in like manner (v9). Let us not rush on, for here is one of the most searching principles Paul describes. Notice the two references to poverty and two references to wealth. Because of our poverty Christ renounced his riches, so that through his poverty we might become rich. It is not material poverty and wealth which Paul has in mind. No, the 'poverty' of Christ is seen in his incarnation and especially his cross, while the 'wealth' he gives us is salvation with all its rich blessings.

As we give, may we, too, reflect on the cross, and all that was achieved for us through the death of Christ. How meagre are our earthly riches in comparison.

4

Christian giving is proportionate giving (8:10–12)

[10]*And here is my advice about what is best for you in this matter: Last year you were the first not only to give but also to have the desire to do so.* [11]*Now finish the work, so that your eager willingness to do it may be matched by your completion of it, according to your means.* [12]*For if the willingness is there, the gift is acceptable according to what one has, not according to what he does not have.*

During the previous year the Corinthian Christians had been the first not only in giving but in desiring to give (v10). So now Paul urges them to finish the task they had begun, so that their doing will keep pace with their desiring. This must be according to their means (v11). For Christian giving is proportionate giving. The eager willingness comes first; so long as that is there, the gift is acceptable in proportion to what the giver has (v12).

This expression 'according to his means' might remind us of two similar expressions which occur in Acts. In Acts 11:29 members of the church in Antioch gave to the famine-stricken Judean Christians 'each according to his ability'. In Acts 2 and 4 members of the church in Jerusalem gave 'to each according to his need'.

Does this ring a bell in our memories? In his *Critique of the Gotha Programme* (1875) Marx called for a society which could 'inscribe on its banners "from each according to his ability" and "to each according to his need"'. I have often wondered if Marx knew these two verses in Acts and if he deliberately borrowed them. Whatever our politics and economics may be, these are certainly biblical principles to which we should hold fast. Christian giving is proportionate giving.

Of course there are times when we are called to give as the Macedonians gave, out of proportion to their income, as a sacrificial offering in particular circumstances. But the principle here is a foundational one. Christian giving should never be less than proportionate to our income.

5

Christian giving contributes to equality (8:13–15)

> [13]*Our desire is not that others might be relieved while you are hard pressed, but that there might be equality.* [14]*At the present time your plenty will supply what they need, so that in turn their plenty will supply what you need. Then there will be equality,* [15]*as it is written: 'He who gathered much did not have too much, and he who gathered little did not have too little.'*

Paul's desire, as he goes on to explain, is not that others may be relieved while they are hard pressed, for that would merely reverse the situation, solving one problem by creating another, but rather 'that there might be equality' (v13). At present, Corinthian plenty will supply the needs of others, so that in turn, at a later stage, the plenty of others will supply Corinthian need. 'Then there will be equality' (v14). Paul illustrates the principle from the supply of manna in the desert. God provided enough for everybody. Larger families gathered a lot, but not too much.

Smaller families gathered less, but not too little, and they had no lack (v15).

Paul is putting the affluence of some alongside the need of others, and calling for an adjustment, that is, an easing of need by affluence.

This was with a view to *isotes*, the Greek word which can mean either 'equality' or 'justice'.

What is this 'equality' for which Paul calls? It has three aspects.

First, it is not egalitarianism. God's purpose is not that everybody receives an identical wage, lives in an identical house, equipped with identical furniture, wears identical clothing and eats identical food—as if we had all been mass-produced in some celestial factory! No. Our doctrine of creation should protect us from any vision of colourless uniformity. For God the Creator has not cloned us. True, we are equal in worth and dignity, equally made in God's image. True, God gives rain and sunshine indiscriminately to both the evil and the good. But God has made us different, and has given his creation a colourful diversity in physique, appearance, temperament, personality and capacities.

Secondly, it begins with equality of educational opportunity. Christians have always been in the forefront of those urging literacy and education for all. For to educate (*educare*) is literally to lead people out into their fullest created potential, so that they may become everything God intends them to be. For example, equal educational opportunity does not mean that every child is sent to university, but that every child capable of benefiting from a university education will be able to have one. No child should be disadvantaged. It is a question of justice.

Thirdly, equality sees an end to extreme social disparity. Julius Nyerere, former President of Tanzania, said in his Arusha Declaration that he wanted to build a nation in which 'no man is ashamed of his poverty in the light of another's affluence, and no man has to be ashamed of his affluence in the light of another's poverty'.

The same dilemma confronts missionaries. Should they 'go native', becoming in all things like the nationals they work among? Or should they continue to enjoy western affluence without any modification of their lifestyle? Probably neither. The Willowbank Report on 'Gospel and Culture' suggests that they should rather develop a standard of living 'which finds it natural to exchange hospitality with others on a basis of reciprocity, without embarrassment' [*The Lausanne Legacy* (Hendrickson/Lausanne 2016)].

If we are embarrassed either to visit other people in their home, or to invite them into ours because of the disparity of our economic lifestyles, something is wrong; the inequality is too great, for it has broken the fellowship. There needs to be a measure of equalization in one or other direction, or in both. And Christian giving contributes to this equality.

6

Christian giving must be carefully supervised (8:16–24)

¹⁶*I thank God, who put into the heart of Titus the same concern I have for you.* ¹⁷*For Titus not only welcomed our appeal, but he is coming to you with much enthusiasm and on his own initiative.* ¹⁸*And we are sending along with him the brother who is praised by all the churches for his service to the gospel.* ¹⁹*What is more, he was chosen by the churches to accompany us as we carry the offering, which we administer in order to honour the Lord himself and to show our eagerness to help.* ²⁰*We want to avoid any criticism of the way we administer this liberal gift.* ²¹*For we are taking pains to do what is right, not only in the eyes of the Lord but also in the eyes of men.*

²²*In addition, we are sending with them our brother who has often proved to us in many ways that he is zealous, and now even more so because of his great confidence in you.* ²³*As for Titus, he is my partner and fellow-worker among you; as for our brothers, they are representatives*

> *of the churches and an honour to Christ.* [24] *There-*
> *fore show these men the proof of your love and*
> *the reason for our pride in you, so that the*
> *churches can see it.*

Handling money is a risky business and Paul is evidently aware of the dangers. He writes 'we want to avoid any criticism of the way we administer this liberal gift' (v20) and 'we are taking pains to do what is right, not only in the eyes of the Lord but also in the eyes of men' (v21). He was determined not only to do right, but to be seen to do right.

So what steps did Paul take? *First*, he did not handle the financial arrangements himself, but put Titus in charge of them (v16–17) and expressed his full confidence in him (v23). *Secondly*, Paul added that he was sending along with Titus another brother, who was 'praised by all the churches for his service to the gospel' (v18). *Thirdly*, this second brother had been 'chosen by the churches to accompany' Paul and carry the gift (v19; 1 Corinthians 16:3). The people carrying the offering to Jerusalem had been elected by the churches because of their confidence in them.

It is wise for us now to take similar precautions against possible criticism. It is good for churches to be openly careful about the number of people present when the offering is counted, and for regular reports to be given to church members on the church finances. We need such transparency in church life; it gives confidence to the membership.

For mission agencies it is important to have a board giving wise and experienced oversight of the financial operations, so that money received from supporters can be invested well and pressed effectively into service. On a broader canvas, we can be thankful for the work of auditors, and for the government's oversight of all charitable giving through the Charity Commission, or its equivalent, which regulates both good practice and good reporting.

7

Christian giving can be stimulated by a little friendly competition (9:1–5)

There is no need for me to write to you about this service to the saints. [2]For I know your eagerness to help, and I have been boasting about it to the Macedonians, telling them that since last year you in Achaia were ready to give; and your enthusiasm has stirred most of them to action. [3]But I am sending the brothers in order that our boasting about you in this matter should not prove hollow, but that you may be ready, as I said you would be. [4]For if any Macedonians come with me and find you unprepared, we—not to say anything about you—would be ashamed of having been so confident. [5]So I thought it necessary to urge the brothers to visit you in advance and finish the arrangements for the generous gift you had promised. Then it will be ready as a generous gift, not as one grudgingly given.

Paul had been boasting to the churches of northern Greece (eg Philippi) about the eagerness of the churches of southern Greece (eg Corinth) to give, and this enthusiasm had stirred the northerners to action (v2). Now Paul is sending the brothers already mentioned to Corinth to ensure that his boasting about the southerners will not prove hollow and that they will be ready as he had said they would be (v3).

For if some northerners were to come south with Paul and find the southerners unprepared, it would be a huge embarrassment. So Paul sent the brothers in advance, to finish the arrangements for their promised gift. Then they would be ready and their gift would be generous and not grudging (v5). First Paul boasted of southern generosity, so that the northerners will give generously. Now he urges the southerners to give generously, so that the northerners will not be disappointed in them.

It is rather delightful to see how Paul plays off the north and the south against each other to stimulate the generosity of both. Competition is a dangerous game to play, especially if it involves publishing the names of donors and the amounts donated. But we can all be stimulated to greater generosity by hearing about the generosity of others.

In some churches the Church Council or elders are invited ahead of the rest of the congregation to pledge first to a church building project, and the total raised (without individual names) is announced before the church gift day. It can build faith for church members to know that their leaders are truly behind these special giving projects, where much sacrificial giving is needed.

8

Christian giving resembles a harvest (9:6–11a)

⁶Remember this: Whoever sows sparingly will also reap sparingly, and whoever sows generously will also reap generously. ⁷Each man should give what he has decided in his heart to give, not reluctantly or under compulsion, for God loves a cheerful giver. ⁸And God is able to make all grace abound to you, so that in all things at all times, having all that you need, you will abound in every good work. ⁹As it is written:

'He has scattered abroad his gifts to the poor: his righteousness endures for ever.'

¹⁰Now he who supplies seed to the sower and bread for food will also supply and increase your store of seed and will enlarge the harvest of your righteousness. ¹¹ᵃYou will be made rich in every way so that you can be generous on every occasion . . .

Two harvest principles are applied here to Christian giving.

First, we reap what we sow. Whoever sows sparingly reaps sparingly, and whoever sows generously reaps generously (v6). 'Sowing' is an obvious picture of giving. What then can we expect to 'reap'? We should not interpret Paul's point too literally, as if he were saying that the more we give the more we will get. No. Each of us should give 'what he has decided in his heart to give', neither reluctantly, nor under compulsion, but rather ungrudgingly, because 'God loves a cheerful giver' (v7). Let's pause for a moment on that phrase 'what he has decided in his heart to give'. There is a sense here of a settled conviction about how much to give; of a decision reached after careful consideration, and always with joy and cheerfulness.

It is good to remind ourselves here of Paul's earlier letter to the Corinthians and his exhortation to systematic giving (1 Corinthians 16:1-3). Everyone should, he said, set aside a sum of money in relation to his income 'on the first day of the week'. Our facility of setting up a bank transfer, for both our church giving and our mission giving, would be very much in keeping with this. We're reminded again here of the importance of 'deciding'. It is rarely necessary to give on the spur of the moment. How much better to take time and seek that settled conviction.

If we give in this spirit, what will happen? What harvest can we expect to reap? The answer is two-fold: (i) 'God is able to make all grace abound to you' so that 'in all things' (not necessarily in material things) you may have all you need, and (ii) you will 'abound in every good work' because your opportunities for further service will increase (v8). As the psalmist says, the consequence of giving to the poor is to have a righteousness which endures for ever (v9; Psalm 112:9).

Secondly, what we reap has a double purpose. It is both for eating and for further sowing. The God of the harvest is concerned not only to alleviate our present hunger, but to make provision for the future. So he supplies both 'bread for food' (immediate consumption) and 'seed to the sower' (to plant when the next season comes round). In the same way God will 'supply and increase your store of seed and will enlarge the harvest of your righteousness' (v10).

These verses are the origin of the concept of 'seed-money', expecting God to multiply a donor's gift. Paul is not teaching a 'prosperity gospel', as some have claimed. True, he promises that 'you will be made rich in every way', but he adds at once that this is 'so that you can be generous on every occasion' (v11a) and so increase your giving. Wealth is with a view to generosity.

9

Christian giving has symbolic significance

There is more to Christian giving than meets the eye. Paul is quite clear about this. In the case of the Greek churches, their giving symbolized their 'confession of the gospel of Christ' (v13). How is that?

Paul looks beyond the mere transfer of cash to what it represents. The significance was more than *geographical* (from Greece to Judea) or *economical* (from the rich to the poor). It is also *theological* (from Gentile Christians to Jewish Christians), for it was a deliberate, self-conscious symbol of Jewish-Gentile solidarity in the body of Christ.

Indeed, this truth (that Jews and Gentiles are admitted to the body of Christ on the same terms, so that in Christ they are heirs together, members together and sharers together) was the 'mystery' which had been revealed to Paul (eg Ephesians 3:1–9). This was the essence of his distinctive gospel. It was the truth he lived for, was imprisoned for and died for. It is hinted at here, but elaborated in Romans 15:25–28.

Paul wrote there that the Gentile churches of Greece had been 'pleased' to make a contribution for the impoverished Christians of Judea. 'They were pleased to do it', he repeated. Indeed 'they owe it to them. For if the Gentiles have shared in the Jews' spiritual blessings [culminating in the coming of the Messiah himself], they owe it to the Jews to share with them their material blessings' (Romans 15:27). It was a striking illustration and declaration of Christian fellowship.

In similar ways, our Christian giving can express our theology. For example, when we contribute to evangelistic enterprises, we are expressing our confidence that the gospel is God's power for salvation, and that everybody has a right to hear it. When we give to economic development, we express our belief that every man, woman and child bears God's image and should not be obliged to live in dehumanizing circumstances. When we give to the maturing of the Church, we acknowledge its centrality in God's purpose and his desire for its maturity.

10

Christian giving promotes thanksgiving to God (9:11b–15)

11b . . . through us your generosity will result in thanksgiving to God.

12 This service that you perform is not only supplying the needs of God's people but is also overflowing in many expressions of thanks to God. 13 Because of the service by which you have proved yourselves, men will praise God for the obedience that accompanies your confession of the gospel of Christ, and for your generosity in sharing with them and with everyone else. 14 And in their prayers for you their hearts will go out to you, because of the surpassing grace God has given you. 15 Thanks be to God for his indescribable gift!

Four times in the concluding paragraph of these two chapters, Paul states his confidence that the ultimate result of their offering will be to increase thanksgiving and praise to God. This is at the heart of all spiritual giving.

> *v11 'your generosity will result in thanksgiving to God'*
>
> *v12 'this service that you perform . . . is . . . overflowing in many expressions of thanks to God'*
>
> *v13 'men will praise God for the obedience that accompanies your confession of the gospel of Christ, and for your generosity'*
>
> *v15 'Thanks be to God for his indescribable gift!'*

Authentic Christian giving leads people not only to thank us, the givers, but to thank God, and to see our gift to them in the light of his indescribable grace, shown supremely in the gift of his Son.

To conclude

It is truly amazing that so much is involved in this transfer of money. We have the doctrine of the Trinity—the grace of God, the cross of Christ and the unity of the Holy Spirit; and we have the practical wisdom of an apostle of Christ. Spiritual truth and practical wisdom both at work, side by side.

What an awesome privilege we have in helping others right across the world to give glory to God. Releasing more of the money which he has entrusted to us as stewards will end in this. And to increase thanksgiving to God for the sake of his own glory is surely our highest goal.

I hope that our study of these chapters will help to raise our giving to a higher level, and will persuade us to give more thoughtfully, more systematically and more sacrificially. I for one (having preached this sermon to myself first) have already reviewed and raised my giving. I venture to hope that you may do likewise.

THE GIFT OF ACCOUNTABILITY

A Short Guide to Financial Accountability

Chris Wright

Author's Preface

To find out what the New Testament teaches about financial accountability in the church, and by extension in all Christian ministry endeavours, let's look at the practice of the Apostle Paul.

There was to be a collection of money from churches in the Roman provinces of Macedonia and Achaia (present-day Greece) to alleviate poverty of other Christians. The money was to be taken to the believers in Jerusalem, where there was evidently a great deal of poverty, and the Apostle Paul oversaw the arrangements. For Paul it was important for one part of the Christian church to help another part in this way.

Paul's references to this collection of money (what he taught about it and the safeguards he put in place) are instructive for us. They show Paul's strong sense of accountability, transparency, and integrity. His example and his teaching apply just as much now, to the financial affairs of churches, missions, and special projects, as they did then.

Paul makes use of the collection as an occasion for teaching. He gives more textual space in his letters to writing about it than he does to writing about justification by faith. That probably surprises us. To state it does not belittle Paul's doctrine of justification or any of his great doctrinal teaching.

We will look at three major passages and a few shorter ones. The major passages are 1 Corinthians 16, where Paul refers to this collection; 2 Corinthians 8–9, where he devotes space to general principles of giving; and Romans 15. (For background: Macedonia is in the northern part of Greece, and the Corinthians, to whom Paul is writing, were in the southern part of Greece, so you will see a kind of north/south rivalry going on.) We see six clear principles at work.

Chris Wright
London

1

Financial *support for the poor* is integral to biblical mission

Paul sees no dichotomy between his evangelistic church-planting mission and his efforts to bring about the relief of poverty among the believers in Jerusalem. Financial support for the poor is a biblical mandate. For Paul this is all part of his task, his mission, and his calling.

Let us step sideways for a moment, to Galatians 2. Here we again see the mandate for the poor. It is not the central focus of Paul's teaching, yet its place in Paul's argument lends particular weight to it. Here Paul is defending three things. He defends (1) his apostolic authority, (2) the content and nature of his apostolic gospel, and (3) the rightness of preaching the gospel to the Gentile Christians, the *Galati*, a branch of the great nations of the Celts that had migrated into southern Turkey. Paul had preached the gospel to them, and they had become believers. Then Paul faced the great theological controversy with the Jewish believers as to how these non-Jewish people could be accepted into the covenant and into the people of God. Some of the Jewish believers had come to Galatia and troubled the Galatian churches, trying to insist that they must become circumcised and observe the Mosaic Law.

Paul writes the Epistle to the Galatians against that background, to defend the fact that his gospel had been accepted as fully authentic by the apostles in Jerusalem. The New Testament church is very young, and it is important for believers to grasp matters clearly. Paul's deep passion for truth and clarity is what lies behind Galatians 2. He declares that he had received his teaching from the Lord but had submitted it to the apostles in Jerusalem, and they had accepted that it was authentic and true. He states:

> *James, Peter, and John, those reputed to be pillars, gave me and Barnabas the right hand of* koinonia—*the right hand of fellowship—when they recognized the grace given to me. They agreed that we should go to the Gentiles, and they to the Jews. All they asked was that we should continue to remember the poor, the very thing I was eager to do. (Galatians 2:9–10)*

The 'right hand of fellowship' is not simply a token of friendship. The word *koinonia* means much more. It is a sharing *in* and a sharing *of* what God has given to us, and that affects the financial dimension as well as the spiritual dimension of our corporate life. So in Acts chapters 2 and 4 we read about the *koinonia* of the early church in Jerusalem. Certainly, it was a spiritual *koinonia*. Believers shared in the apostles' teaching, in the breaking of bread, and in prayers. But it was also a financial *koinonia*; they shared with one another to relieve poverty. It is clear from what Paul says in Galatians 2 that this spirit of the church in Jerusalem was still operating; the Jerusalem church still cared about the poor in their midst. They saw it as an essential part of gospel *koinonia*. So if Paul the apostle was going to be a partner with them and share in their understanding of the gospel, then he too must be committed to remembering the poor as part of his gospel credentials. It was, he says, the very thing he was eager to do anyway. So we learn that active financial concern for the poor is how the Jerusalem church operated, and it was part of Paul's commitment.

At the end of Paul's letter to the church in Rome (Romans 15), Paul writes about his lifelong commitment to church planting and evangelistic ministry. Earlier in the chapter he explained how God had given him grace 'to be a minister of Christ Jesus to the Gentiles with the priestly duty of proclaiming the gospel of God,' so that the Gentiles were becoming an offering to God (vv 15–16). That is his ministry, and that is what he believes he is called to do. He has now done it all around the eastern Mediterranean basin, from Jerusalem to Illyricum (now modern Albania). He continues:

> *I have fully proclaimed the gospel of Christ. It has always been my ambition to preach the gospel where Christ was not known, so that I would not be building on someone else's foundation. . . . But now . . . there is no more place for me to work in these regions. (vv 19–20, 23)*

So now Paul is planning a bold missionary project that will take him to the western half of the Mediterranean, toward Spain. That is his great evangelistic vision, and he is looking forward to visiting the Christians in Rome on the way. But *at the moment*, says Paul, my priority is to go to Jerusalem in the service of the saints there. 'For Macedonia and Achaia were pleased to make a contribution for the poor among the saints in Jerusalem. They were pleased to do it, and indeed they owe it to them. For if the Gentiles have shared in the Jews' spiritual blessings, they owe it to the Jews to share with them their material blessings. So after I have completed this task and have made sure that they have received this fruit, I will go to Spain and visit you on the way. I know that when I come to you, I will come in the full measure of the blessing of Christ' (vv 26–29).

Look carefully at what he says a bit later: 'Pray that I may be rescued from the unbelievers in Judea and that my service in Jerusalem may be acceptable to the saints there, so that by God's will I may come to you with joy and together with you be refreshed' (vv 31–32).

Paul in effect puts his evangelistic strategy on hold, to carry out his *relief of poverty strategy*. It is interesting that at this point Paul does not say, 'I've got to go on to evangelize Spain, so I'll dump the responsibility for this financial gift onto somebody else; they can take it to Jerusalem. My job is to preach the gospel, not to relieve the poor.' Paul sees no conflict in making his priority at this point his service to the saints through the relief of poverty. So first he will take the collected money to the people in Jerusalem. Not only does he see it as a personal priority; he asks for prayer for it. He asks for prayer just as later he would ask for prayer when he was in prison (when he asked people to pray for courage to preach the gospel). Just as he called on believers to pray for him in his evangelistic ministry, here he asks the Roman Christians to pray for him in his financial ministry to the saints in Jerusalem.

He does not perceive this task as an unavoidable interruption in his evangelistic career. To complete this work of poverty-relief will be to fulfil a Christ-centred calling; as much so as when he was completing his evangelistic mandate. When he has done this, he says, 'I will come to you in the full measure of Christ'. What a rich phrase, carrying with it a deep sense of fulfilling Christ's calling.

Paul sees no dichotomy between these two dimensions of ministry. Indeed, as one writer has said, 'We do not know if Paul achieved this mission [his evangelistic plans to go to Spain], but we do know that he delivered the collection [to relieve the poor in Jerusalem]. *The collection was so vital that its delivery was at that moment a more urgent matter for Paul than his desire to evangelize and plant churches on the missionary frontier*.'[1]

In 1 Timothy 6 Paul instructs Timothy to pass this teaching on to the church. The responsibility for generous giving by those who have the means is core to our Christian commitment and part of our response to the gospel. Paul says,

> *Command those who are rich in this present world not to be arrogant nor to put their hope in wealth, which is so uncertain, but to put their hope in God, who richly provides us with everything for our enjoyment. Command them [note this second use of 'command'] to do good, to be rich in good deeds, and to be generous and willing to share. (1 Timothy 6:17–18)*

1. Jason Hood, 'Theology in Action: Paul and Christian Social Care', in *Transforming the World: The Gospel and Social Responsibility*, ed. Jamie A. Grant and Dewi A. Hughes (Nottingham: IVP Apollos, 2009), pp 129–46. Quotation taken from p 134; italics original.

The English conceals the fact that the Greek word is *koinonikos* ['willing to share']. They are to share their fellowship by their financial generosity, and in this way they will lay up treasure for themselves as a firm foundation for the coming age, echoing the teaching of Jesus.

Generosity is a Christian duty, says Paul, something that pastors can command. He is probably echoing Deuteronomy 15, where God says to the Israelites (vv 10–11, 14–15),

> *Give generously to him [the poor person] and do so without a grudging heart; then because of this the LORD your God will bless you. . . . There will always be poor people in the land [or in the world]. Therefore I command you to be open-handed toward your brothers. . . . Give to him [that is, the poor person] as the LORD your God has blessed you. Remember that you were slaves in Egypt and the LORD your God redeemed you. That is why I give you this command today.*

Summary Principle 1: Paul saw generous financial support for the poor and careful administration of that gift as integral to biblical mission, gospel mission. It was part of what he was called to do, as well as the more obviously evangelistic tasks of preaching and planting churches.

2

Financial *administration* is a stewardship of grace and obedience

When we handle money given by God's people, we are handling (1) the fruit of God's grace and (2) practical proof of human obedience to the gospel. Money that has been given as an offering to God is not just 'stuff'. It is not just coins and notes or covenants or ledgers or entries in a journal. When we handle money that has been given by God's people, we are involved in a deeply spiritual matter. God's people give in response to God's kindness. As we handle that money we are entrusted with something; we are stewards of the fruit of grace in their lives and stewards of the proof of obedience.

This understanding of our stewardship comes from what Paul says at the beginning of chapter 8 and the end of chapter 9 of 1 Corinthians. Notice how frequently the word 'grace' occurs in these familiar words.

Now, brothers, we want you to know about the grace that God has given the Macedonian churches. Out of the most severe trial, their overflowing joy and their extreme poverty welled up in rich generosity. For I testify that they gave as much as they were able, and even beyond their ability. Entirely on their own, they urgently pleaded with us for the privilege of sharing in this service to the saints. And they did not do as we expected, but they gave themselves first to the Lord and then to us in keeping with God's will. So we urged Titus, since he had earlier made a beginning, to bring also to completion this act of grace on your part. But just as you excel in everything—in faith, in speech, in knowledge, in complete earnestness and in your love for us— see that you also excel in this grace of giving. (2 Corinthians 8:1–7)

Three times Paul uses the word 'grace' about the Macedonian believers, and a couple of verses later he talks about 'the *grace* of our Lord Jesus Christ.' Note that the word *koinonia* is in there again. This desire to give was a mark of their *koinonia*, their fellowship.

This gift of the Macedonians, Paul writes, was a response to the Lord ('they gave themselves first to the Lord'). Moreover, it was something that they wanted to do. They did not have to be asked to give; they asked for the privilege of giving. Because of the grace of God in them, they responded in an act of grace to others. This is reciprocal grace, or grace being expressed in action.

Paul sends Titus to oversee and administer the collection. It is as if Paul was saying (and I think this is slightly the flavour of his wording), 'Because this is such an important evidence of the grace of God and of the fruit of the gospel in the lives of these believers, I am sending my most trusted senior person to handle this responsibility'. He did not send a junior clerk or some young functionary who might be haphazard in dealing with it all. Paul says, in effect, 'It is a serious matter, so we urged Titus—an apostolic delegate in the church—to go and make sure that it was properly handled and treated with the seriousness it deserves'.

This display of generosity was not just an act of grace, but also an act of obedience.

> *This service that you perform is not only supplying the needs of God's people but is also overflowing in many expressions of thanks to God. Because of the service by which you [that is, you Gentiles] have proved yourselves, men will praise God for the obedience that accompanies your confession of the gospel of Christ, and for your generosity in sharing with them [koinonia again] and with everyone else. And in their*

*prayers for you their hearts will go out to you
because of the surpassing grace God has given
you. (2 Corinthians 9:12–15)*

And, Paul adds, 'Thanks be to God for *his*
indescribable gift!' which of course is the Lord
Jesus Christ.

According to Paul giving, sharing, and generosity are not just grace; they are also proof of
obedience. Why was that important? Precisely
because these were Gentiles. The Jewish believers
in Jerusalem were still uncertain whether or not
these Gentiles, who had never been circumcised
and were not keeping the Law, were really part of
the family. Did they really belong to the covenant
people of God? Paul responds, 'The fact that you
Gentiles have given an offering to meet the needs
of Jewish believers is a proof of the fellowship
that we have in Christ. Your obedience to the
gospel is a demonstration that though you have
been so despised by the Jews historically, you are
now at one with them; that there is no difference,
there is no Jew or Gentile, male or female, slave
or free'. Let's not miss the profound significance
here. This gift was a proof of obedience to the
core meaning of the gospel.

*Summary Principle 2: Handling a gift offered by
God's people is a sacred trust. Administering it is*

a stewardship of the grace of God and of the obe-dience of God's people to the gospel. Paul's concern for accountability, integrity, and transparency was not just to satisfy the Roman governors or other officials. It arose because he was dealing with something coming from God: the grace of God and obedience to the gospel.

3

Financial *appeals* require advance planning

Look how thoroughly Paul prepares the way for the gift. In 1 Corinthians he has been answering a lot of questions from the church, and he comes back to something that he has told them about before, but wants to raise again. He wants them to be ready and prepared.

Now about the collection for God's people: Do what I told the Galatian churches to do. On the first day of every week, each one of you should set aside a sum of money in keeping with his income, saving it up, so that when I come no collections will have to be made. Then, when I arrive, I will give letters of introduction to the men you approve and send them with your gift to Jerusalem. (1 Corinthians 16:1–3)

In 2 Corinthians 9:1–5 Paul shows the same concern for preparedness.

There is no need for me to write to you about this service to the saints. For I know your eagerness to help, and I have been boasting about it to the Macedonians, telling them that since last year you in Achaia were ready to give [again catch the note of north/south rivalry]; and your enthusiasm has stirred most of them to action. But I am sending the brothers [that is, I am sending some people in advance] in order that our boasting about you in this matter should not prove hollow, but that you may be ready, as I said you would be. For if any Macedonians come with me and find you unprepared, we . . . would be ashamed of having been so confident. So I thought it necessary to urge the brothers to visit you in advance and finish the arrangements for the generous gift you had promised. Then it will be ready as a generous gift, not as one grudgingly given (that is, pulled together at the last minute).

Can you see what Paul is doing here? He does not want this collection to become debased into an emotional appeal in which everybody is urged to put their hands in their pockets, and the music goes on until everybody has dug deeper, and then the offering buckets are sent around again. No, Paul is purposely avoiding that type of emotional manipulation. He does not want there to be any kind of 'on-the-spot' pressure for a gift that has not been carefully thought through. Paul wants his collection and the giving by the church to be something that has been thought about, prayed

about, and prepared for. It should be systematic
(we should plan what we will give); it should be
regular (week by week setting money aside); it
should be proportionate (according to income,
with those who have more giving more); the
means of collecting should be transparent (the
brothers will come and they will oversee it); and
the total collected should be public (announced
and recorded). All of this preparation and super-
vision is built into Paul's careful planning.

Accountability is not just an afterthought;
it is not something you try to sort out after the
event—'All this money has come in, how won-
derful! Now we'd better decide what we do with
it, who is going to count it, who is going to bank
it, and who will keep accounts'. Accountability
is not just a matter of reacting when problems
arise. It should be planned; it should be built in
from the very start. Paul says, 'Look, here is what
we are planning. This is what we're asking *you* to
do, and this is what *we* will then do when you
have done what we ask'. The whole procedure
is a matter of shared responsibility. Paul does
not want their giving to be mere opportunism:
'Paul's come to town again; let's have a quick collection and give him a love gift'. No, Paul wants
this offering to be carefully thought through and
planned well in advance, so that nobody will be
taken by surprise and nobody can be accused of

emotional manipulation. That is an important way by which he builds accountability into his financial relationship with the church.

Notice that Paul is concerned, also, about loss of face. The world of ancient Greece and Rome is a relational economy, so he conducts this offering relationally. He says, 'Some of our brothers will be coming to you, and I will be coming later as well, and we don't want any embarrassment. I don't want you to lose face; I don't want you to be ashamed, and I don't want them to be gloating. So let's do this properly, and let's plan it and have it all out on the table clear and open, so that everybody is satisfied'.

Summary Principle 3: Proper planning of financial appeals is important, and safeguards should be set up before the event.

4

Financial *temptations* call for 'safety in numbers'

Wherever there is money, there is temptation. This is just as true for Christians as anybody else, so it is wise to protect ourselves from temptation by having more than one person involved in handling the money. This way of working was true of Paul's ministry in general. He was a great individual minister, preacher, gospel letter writer, and everything else. But generally he did not operate alone. He was the leader, but he worked with teams that included people such as Silas, Barnabas, Timothy, and Titus. Indeed, when Paul did find himself completely alone, he was distressed about it. In 2 Timothy 4:16 there are heartrending words when everyone has deserted him; this was terrible for him. He wanted to be in a team; he wanted to belong with others.

Great emphasis is laid on the plurality of people involved in handling money. Knowing exactly who was involved becomes quite complicated, but evidently there were several people.

In 1 Corinthians 16:3–4 Paul says, 'I will give letters of introduction to the men you approve'— in other words, those whom the Christians in Corinth trusted. Then offering to do the task himself, he writes, 'If it seems advisable for me to go also, they will accompany me.' So he would not take charge of the money by himself, but would involve others.

It is also difficult to know how many are involved in 2 Corinthians 8:16–24, but we can identify some.

> *I thank God, who put into the heart of Titus the same concern I have for you. For Titus not only welcomed our appeal, but he is coming to you with much enthusiasm and on his own initiative. And we are sending along with him the brother who is praised by all the churches for his service to the gospel [this was a trusted Christian leader]. What is more, he was chosen by the churches to accompany us.*

So he was someone elected or chosen and appointed to exercise this financial responsibility. In addition to this, 'We are sending with them our brother [Paul does not name him] who has often proved to us in many ways that he is zealous, and now even more so because of his great confidence in you' (v 22).

So the point is, certainly more than one person was involved, and they were all trusted people. They were accepted and known by everybody. There was no anonymity. Christian accountability is a matter of trust between fellow believers, but Paul shows us the wisdom of building in safeguards of plurality, because even believers are still sinners and few things are more tempting than money. Paul is well aware that even trusted brothers can go astray. Sadly, we read about a few of them at the end of his letters when he writes that some who preferred the world and the world's ways have gone off and left him (e.g., 2 Timothy 4:10). Paul knew that even the best people need the protection of relational accountability to one another.

So then, Paul insists on plurality in the handling of money. It is a very wise principle to adopt in any church or Christian endeavour. In many UK churches, certainly in my own church at All Souls, gift money is never counted by only one person. When the offering is brought to the vestry, there are always at least two and sometimes three or four people in the room. The door is then closed, and they count the offering together. They are a check on one another. Now of course, we all trust one another; nobody expects that anybody is going to be doing anything wrong, but there is need for openness and verifiability in handling money. We need to be above suspicion.

Many organizations, including my own, will not allow bank cheques to be signed by only one person; there must always be two signatories to manage the bank account and the finances. That is another wise practice.

How do we make that work in a cultural setting where it is unthinkable to question the honour and authority of the senior leader—least of all by calling him to account over money? That would be to break the relationship and cause loss of face. So how should we ensure proper accountability? Perhaps here the leaders themselves should take the initiative. They could choose to say, 'Please, will you join me as we do this? I request that other people should be involved with me as we arrange our financial affairs, or as we handle these funds, or as we set up this Trust. I want other people alongside myself to see how the money is handled and how the decisions are made. I want them to be completely satisfied that all is being done transparently and honourably'. In that way the person at the top is able to lead from the top and to set the example, just as the Apostle Paul did. Paul could easily have said, 'I'm an apostle. Trust me. I'll do this myself'. But he did not. He insisted *from the top* that there should be others alongside him to ensure it was all done honestly. If a leader does this *voluntarily*, he is not saying to those under him, 'I think you don't trust me'. Rather he is saying, 'I know you trust me. And because you trust me, I want to make sure that your trust is never betrayed. I want to be completely transparent, and therefore I choose to share my accountability with other trusted Christian friends and brothers'.

Summary Principle 4: To introduce higher standards of accountability, we must lead by example. Accountability is something we as leaders should choose to have, for our own good and for the protection of the Lord's name, not something that is forced upon us.

5

Financial *accountability* demands transparency before God and man

I love the fact that when Paul has finished talking about all the people he is bringing into the team to deliver the money to Jerusalem, he explains why he is handling it in this plural way.

We want to avoid any criticism of the way we administer this liberal gift. For we are taking pains to do what is right, not only in the eyes of the Lord, but also in the eyes of men. (2 Corinthians 8:20–21)

These verses express a principle that is transcultural. That is, they provide a biblical model for us, whatever our culture or background. They are challenging and very significant. I think they should be hung up on the wall of any room where a Christian organization does its financial business.

The arrangements Paul put in place were not only very careful but also probably quite costly. It would cost a lot more for five or six men to travel from Greece to Jerusalem than for Paul to go there by himself; travel was not cheap in those days. So the arrangements Paul was building up around this gift could have aroused resistance. Church members could have said, 'Why send so many people? You are going to waste some of the gift on their expenses' (just as we complain about the cost of auditing our accounts). But Paul says, 'It's worth that cost because I don't want any criticism; I want to be completely transparent before God and people, so that nothing we do can be open to criticism'.

Paul was operating within a culture that had similarities to some non-Western cultures today. The Greek and Roman cultures were very top-down, very hierarchical. The Roman system was patron-client oriented. The men at the top were patrons: they were bankers or politicians; they were wealthy, and people would come to their homes every day wanting favours. Being in with the top man was crucially important; that is how Roman politics worked. It was a very relational economy in that sense.

So Paul is acting counterculturally in what he does with this gift. He could have said, 'I'm the boss; I'm your patron; I'm the apostle. Give me the money and a single armed guard, and I'll take it to Jerusalem. Just trust me'. Instead he says, 'No, I want this to be completely transparent, so

I must have others with me to make sure all is done properly and above criticism'.

I would love 2 Corinthians 8:21 to become a motto for each of us as Christ's followers; something that we take to heart: 'We are taking pains to do what is right, not only in the eyes of the Lord, but also in the eyes of men'. Let us make this principle a motto for each of us and for all our mission organizations. What a difference it could make, and how it could help to prevent some of the tragic scandals of fraud and theft and mismanagement within Christian organizations.

Summary Principle 5: The vertical and the horizontal are both needed. Paul says, 'We should be able to trust one another in the Lord, but we want to do what is beyond criticism in the eyes of the watching world as well'.

6

Financial *trustworthiness* is an apostolic honour to Christ

Let's look at upward and downward accountability. We tend to think that we are *upwardly* accountable to bodies such as boards and funding foundations and donors and the government and legal authorities, and *downwardly* accountable to our beneficiaries, that is, to those who actually receive from our ministry, those whom we are serving. However, the direction of our accountability is the reverse. Our *upward* accountability is to those who occupy the position Jesus was referring to when he said, 'Inasmuch as you do it to the least of these my brethren, you do it for me' (see Matthew 25:40). Those our ministry is serving are actually Jesus to us. So our accountability to them is really our accountability to him—which is 'upward'. When we serve others in our ministry, we are serving Christ. We are honouring him in serving them.

Paul says in several passages that discharging this financial responsibility in a trustworthy manner is an honour to Christ, not just a matter of transparency before men. It was important to do the job with honesty and integrity. But even more, it was important to do it for the honour and glory of Christ. Look first at 2 Corinthians 8:18–19. Who were these people who were administering the gift? Paul says, 'We are sending along with him [Titus] the brother who is praised by all the churches for his service to the gospel. What is more, he was chosen by the churches'. Titus was an honoured person whose life was already seen to be honouring to the Lord and honouring to the gospel, and therefore Paul and the Corinthians could trust him with their money. And the way he handles the money will also be honouring to the Lord and to the church. Honest finances are honouring to Christ (with the obvious implication that dishonesty dishonours Christ).

The point is even more explicit in verses 23 and 24.

> *As for Titus, he is my partner and fellow worker among you; as for our brothers, they are representatives of the churches and an honour to Christ. Therefore show these men the proof of your love and the reason for our pride in you, so that the churches can see it.*

The word 'representatives', used there, is actually *apostoloi*, apostles. It is used in the weaker sense that occurs several times in the New Testament to refer to others beyond the twelve apostolic pillars of the church (the twelve disciples, minus Judas Iscariot and plus Matthias in the Book of Acts, and then the Apostle Paul). In this slightly looser sense, the word *apostolos* meant someone who was an emissary or a trusted delegate of the churches. There seem to have been a number of these apostolic delegates—Titus, Timothy, and others who are mentioned in 3 John and elsewhere. So Paul says, these *apostoloi*, these chosen delegates of the churches who are being entrusted with the responsibility of handling finances within the churches, especially this large financial gift to Jerusalem, are an honour to Christ.

What a commendation! What a way to speak of an accountant or treasurer! These people are entrusted with money. And by being faithful in that trust, they are not only an honour to Christ, but also they should have church approval (v 24): 'Show these men the proof of your love', because we want them to be seen by all the churches.

Look at how Paul speaks about Epaphroditus in Philippians 2:25–30. He says, 'I think it is necessary to send back to you Epaphroditus, my brother, fellow worker and fellow soldier, who is also your messenger.' Again the word is *apostolos*, your apostle. Epaphroditus was not an apostle in the sense that Paul was, but he was the emissary, the representative, the trusted messenger of the church, and hence apostolic. Paul continues,

> *whom you sent to take care of my needs. For he longs for all of you and is distressed because you heard he was ill. Indeed he was ill, and almost died. But God had mercy on him, and not on him only but also on me, to spare me sorrow upon sorrow. Therefore I am all the more eager to send him [back]. . . . Welcome him in the Lord with great joy, and honor men like him, because he almost died for the work of Christ, risking his life to make up for the help you could not give me.*

What Paul is describing is Epaphroditus's handling of the financial and material gift that the Philippian church had made to Paul when Paul was in need. And Paul says in effect, 'That service of Epaphroditus was a work of the gospel; that was a work born out of love for Christ and for his church. Epaphroditus nearly died doing what he did and, therefore,' Paul says, 'honour him. What he is doing, he is doing for Christ's sake'.

In Philippians 4:14–19 we find another reference to the same thing, the gift that was sent to Paul through Epaphroditus. Verse 18 reads, 'I have received full payment and even more; I am amply supplied, now that I have received from Epaphroditus the gifts you sent. They are a fragrant offering, an acceptable sacrifice, pleasing to God.' Epaphroditus's role then, says Paul, was an apostolic honour: serving God and serving Christ by serving the servants of God. In serving the servants of God, people like Epaphroditus are deserving of honour and respect, because they are an honour to Christ himself.

To administer financial affairs with trustworthiness, with transparency, with honesty as did Epaphroditus and others in the New Testament, is a Christ-honouring thing to do: we do it for him.

When I was the principal of All Nations Christian College near London, there was a time when issues arose that affected me personally. The chairman of the college Board of Directors was a very wise, godly brother whom I greatly respected. I was required to give account of some aspects of how I was running things and reasons for decisions that had been made. That was not easy; it is not comfortable to have people poking into everything that is going on. That is true even if you have nothing troubling your conscience. I knew that in relation to the college I had done nothing wrong, but still I had to accept the questioning. At one point, the chairman of the Council said, 'Chris, accountability is not a burden; it's a *gift*. It's a gift that we give you. We hold you accountable, and that is for your good; it's for your protection. It's not something we are imposing upon you. It's something we are *giving* to you because we love you, because you are a brother in Christ, and we want to affirm your integrity by expecting proper accountability'. I thought that was a very helpful, positive way for me to look at the demanding challenge of accountability. I learned to see it, not as a threat or an insult or 'beneath my dignity to be questioned', but as something that was honouring to me and also, of course, to God.

Summary Principle 6: In 1 Samuel 2:30 God said through a prophet to Eli, 'Those who honor me I will honor'. If we want the Lord's honour, we need to be honourable in the way we handle money and in the way we hold ourselves accountable; we need to be transparent men and women of integrity in everything. Let us make Paul and his teaching on this matter a powerful and authoritative model for ourselves.

May we all pray for God to grant us the courage to live and work with complete integrity, and may we honour one another by expecting— and giving—accountability to one another and to the Lord.

Questions for Reflection

What steps can you take to help your church sustain practical concern for the poor in (1) your locality? (2) your nation? (3) the world?

Are there more safeguards your church or ministry should put in place to protect those who handle money?

Appeal letters should state needs openly and not exaggerate past triumphs or future possibilities. Long-term spiritual ministry does not always see exciting results. If your church members or your donors respond only to exciting stories, how can you help them grasp this?

Treasurers and Finance Committee members, like all spiritual leaders, must be men and women of Christian character. In addition they need relevant gifting and experience. Does your church or ministry have good structures in place (1) for appointing these officers? (2) for their reporting to (a) the leadership? (b) the membership?

Recommended Reading

From the Lausanne Movement

The Cape Town Commitment: A Call to Action. A Study Guide for Small Groups. Compiled by Sara Singleton and Matt Ristuccia (Hendrickson Publishers)

The Cape Town Commitment: Study Edition. A Confession of Faith and a Call to Action by Rose Dowsett (Hendrickson Publishers)

Ephesians: Studying with the Global Church by Lindsay Olesberg. Participant's Guide (Hendrickson Publishers)

Creation Care and the Gospel. Lausanne Consult 1. Edited by Colin Bell and Robert S White (Hendrickson Publishers)

The Glory of the Cross by James Philip (Hendrickson Publishers)

Lausanne Movement

Connecting influencers and ideas for global mission

The Lausanne Movement takes its name from the International Congress on World Evangelization, convened in 1974 in Lausanne, Switzerland, by the US evangelist Billy Graham. His long-time friend John Stott, the UK pastor-theologian, was chief architect of *The Lausanne Covenant*, which issued from this gathering.

Two further global Congresses followed—the second in Manila, Philippines (1989) and the third in Cape Town, South Africa (2010). From the Third Lausanne Congress came *The Cape Town Commitment: A Confession of Faith and a Call to Action*. Its Call to Action was the fruit of a careful process conducted over four years to discern what we believe the Holy Spirit is saying to the global church in our times. In the words of the *Commitment*'s chief architect, Chris Wright, it expresses 'the conviction of a Movement and the voice of a multitude.'

The Lausanne Movement connects evangelical influencers across regions and across generations: in the church, in ministries and in the workplace. Under God, Lausanne events have often acted as a powerful catalyst; as a result, strategic ideas such as Unreached People Groups, the 10/40 Window, and holistic/integral mission have been introduced to missional thinking. Over 30 specialist Issue Networks now focus on the outworking of the priorities outlined in *The Cape Town Commitment.*

The movement makes available online over 40 years of missional content. Sign up to receive *Lausanne Global Analysis* to your inbox. Watch videos from Lausanne's gatherings. On the website you will also find a complete list of titles in the Lausanne Library.

www.lausanne.org